Äiti

poems by

Alexa Gutter

Finishing Line Press
Georgetown, Kentucky

Äiti

ACKNOWLEDGMENTS

Grateful acknowledgement is made to *Glassworks Magazine*, in which an
earlier form of "Top of the Stairs, Looking Down" appeared.

To my husband Aaron and our children Julian and Elias, thank you for your
love and support. You are the reason for everything.

To my sister Alana and my father Mark, thank you for both reading and
inhabiting these poems with me. You are a much cherished part of this story.

To Amy Bernard, many thanks for your beautiful art and for championing
my poetry.

To Nancy K. Pearson, wonderful poet and teacher, thank you for your
guidance and encouragement.

And to the Bucks County Poets, especially the late Christopher Bursk, thank
you for reading and critiquing many of these poems in their original forms. I
will always remember your generosity and community.

Publisher: Leah Huete de Maines
Editor: Christen Kincaid
Cover Art: Amy Bernard
Author Photo: Crissy Everhart
Cover Design: Elizabeth Maines McCleavy

Order online: www.finishinglinepress.com
also available on amazon.com

Author inquiries and mail orders:
Finishing Line Press
PO Box 1626
Georgetown, Kentucky 40324
USA

Contents

For Aila

Top of the Stairs, Looking Down

You were ten, bundled for Finnish winter,
standing at the brink of cement steps, when

Mirja, neighbor-girl, school-friend, stretched
her woolen hands in front of her and shoved.

How many stairs? In your story, the drop
seemed endless, the concrete icy, unforgiving.

I could see it clearly: little girl you crumpled in
a heap of boots and knitted clothes, your white

mitten blood-soaked as you touched the place
where your cheek had broken open. And Mirja!

Mirja at the top of the stairs, rosy face glowing
with pleasure, unmoved by the reddening snow.

I learned all this when I asked about
the pale scar just above your cheekbone,

near the outer corner of your left eye,
a place where tears collect and spill over.

At five, the injustice of it rattled me, outraged
me each time I looked at the spidery mark.

In Helsinki that summer, we sat with Mirja
and her daughters at an outdoor café as though

the whole betrayal had never occurred.
How was it that such a villain should grow up,

have children, eat cups of vanilla ice cream?
How strange to discover you were once a small girl.

How bewildering to find out years later
that you would not live forever,

that I might touch your swollen face and
you wouldn't feel it, wouldn't open your eyes.

Forget How You Learned to Swim

Those early lessons don't matter now,
at three in the morning, in the back seat of a car
on a dirt road in central Finland.
A little drunk, you've been quiet all night,
but now you shout in Finnish:
>   *We shall all go swimming!*
It sounds like dialogue between Matti and Anna
in a dated textbook; your companions laugh.
This is Äiti's country. Familiar
and foreign, just like her.
She has always been your guidebook,
your translator, and tonight she isn't here.
She would caution against such a jaunt,
knows the pull of dark water,
drove you to swimming class on Saturdays
just so you could learn to float.
There is a nearby lake, of course,
a worn dock that feels smooth underfoot.
You toss your sundress over a tree stump.
At twenty, your body is small and ready,
slim neck hasn't been kissed in months.
You walk as though balancing a cup too full,
and stare down to black waves
lapping at a wooden ladder.
Splashes echo in a soundless night,
and you are plunged into a cold silk
which billows around you.
The orange sky releases you,
draws you suddenly up.

Varkaus, Finland

When the clouds opened
we were on our way to the evening market.
I don't remember what summer it was,
maybe I was six, Alana ten, and we
were hoping for ice cream with berries.

That town, our mother's birthplace,
smelled like sodden newsprint when it rained.
She had run half across the world
to clear the scent of paper mills from her nose,
but I could only sense forest, damp earth.

We rode with strangers who stopped for us:
two handsome men with smiles for my mother.
In the back seat, she grasped our hands
and whispered *Don't tell Mummi*
like hitchhiking had made her sixteen again.

On the way home, we sprinted, clothing soaked,
her mascara running in tiny black rivers,
our sneakers sloshing rhythms in the mud.
Just daughters then, all of us,
three slick brown heads shining with rain.

1973: My Mother Visits her Hometown

"I am very strange, crazy, and a big zero, and all the other
unpleasant things one can think of. I've known it all my life..."
—*letter from my mother to my father, 1973*

At night, she slides three blue ballpoint
covered sheets in an envelope marked airmail.
August in Finland: outside the kitchen window
there are still haloes of light around the trees.

Tomorrow she'll walk to the post office, she'll
keep her head down so no one recognizes her,
no one asks. She's beautiful, the world has told her.
Keith Moon asked her out and she said no.

The girl at the post office will offer a thin smile
of acknowledgement—will not utter
the grade-school nickname that flickers
in her thoughts. *She's blonde now*

she'll whisper later, *married an American.*
The woman who is not my mother yet
will exit the post office. *I am a big zero,*
she will think as the door swings open.

When we were 4 and 8

You took our hands and told us about loss,
your sister in her crib gone still one night.
In black and white a photo showed us how
the small coffin was placed in frozen ground.
You were not there. No, you were only two.
Who kept you then? Who sat you in a chair
in some warm kitchen with a slice of bread?
One summer we took pansies to her grave
and Mummi walked ahead, she knew the way.
Years after that you told me of your dream
that Eija had grown up with light blonde hair.
She reached for you; you held her in your arms.
I guess we never balanced what you'd lost,
the girls you made, your sister made of dust.

Self-Portrait in an Airplane

After Adam Zagajewski

Knees hugged to chest
I am egg-shaped in
my narrow seat

remembering that
first easy flight
when I was six,

head heavy in
my mother's lap,
I slept for hours—

thirty thousand
feet in the air
and full of trust.

Now, my heart
is afraid of itself.
My blood pumps

with pills and wine
drunk hastily
in an airport bar.

I curl my body tight,
press my forehead
hard against my knees.

A monk wrapped in orange
robes sits behind me,
serene, wanting nothing.

I desire too much,
am never satisfied.
Sleep does not come.

Grade School

Disheveled, red-faced, hurtling myself
away from the school bus,
I was desperate to come home—
the quiet coolness, my mother's hands.

What happened, she'd say
to me, examining my drawn face.
I had no reply. Too much happened,
like always:

wild shrieks of children
at recess, dull pencils, my bad handwriting.
I drew a picture of my mother
and began to cry. They sent me to the nurse.

My life was full of tiny emergencies
sewn together like a misshapen quilt.
My head ached every afternoon, until
I could sit alone and stare and think.

I wonder about that child
as I walk to my car, high heels percussive
on pavement. I catch a glimpse
of myself in the shiny window of a Volvo:

hair out of place, eyeliner smudged.
When do I stop being her?
When do I become something
strong and lovely?

Staying Home

There were days I went to school
only to come right home again.
At thirteen, I begged my mother
to let me stay in bed mornings

when my hands shook
with inexplicable terror.
She was desperate for my courage,
so I walked numbly to the bus stop.

When she picked me up later
she wasn't angry,
though wrinkles of resignation
had sprouted between her brows.

She didn't try to cheer me up.
We never went out for sundaes or
watched old comedies to pass
the heavy hours of afternoon.

Once home I'd slip under cool covers
and close my swollen eyes.
At noon I'd unpack the sandwich
meant for the cafeteria's noise,

a squished brown thing with
thin, hardened peanut butter.
Upstairs, my mother worried.
I fished carrot sticks out of a Ziploc bag.

Sanctuary

I.

When I was small my mother would take me to Princeton Chapel to admire the stained-glass windows. I could tell she liked them very much, because her breath would change as she looked at them—a sharp intake, sometimes a sigh. She was teaching me about beauty. We were always alone, we always whispered. I must have been three. I remember squinting as we left the church; the sun seemed too sudden, the cars on Nassau Street far from sacred.

II.

I am sitting, with my new husband, in the empty pews of a medieval church in Montalcino. All we can hear is the wind and an owl hooting, incessantly, demanding to be noticed. La civetta, he says, naming it in Italian to teach me. I do not say anything in response, and we are silent for a long time. Outside we hear the echoing call of a child to his mother, but we cannot make out what he says. In the darkness, I whisper the last lines of some old poem.

III.

I light a candle for my mother in the Basilica San Domenico, where the preserved head of St. Catherine hovers in a gilded frame. I stare at the stained-glass portrait of Jesus above the altar, and try to find solace there—in his glowing turquoise eyes. Through the window, a flash of lightning is followed by thunder so loud I jump. I don't bother to wipe the trio of tears from my face, feeling their individual journeys down my cheek and neck, until they finally rest somewhere underneath my shirt. My mother is not here, in this church. I stand at the door, letting a line of French tourists pass me. Wrapped in plastic rain ponchos, they step into the insistent downpour.

Mr. Gull

When we were small, it seemed that Mr. Gull
prowled in shadows of the house,
that if we didn't stay sharp, he might
step out from behind a corner, sneering.

"Don't answer the doorbell," my father warned
if we were home alone, because Mr. Gull
made a habit of unplanned visits. And though
it could've been the mailman, better to be safe.

If I picked up the phone to emptiness,
a rapid click, a breathless wrong number,
that was surely the work of Mr. Gull,
who was not much of a conversationalist.

Once, he stole a doll's shoe and never returned it.
He must have done it just to be mean,
placing it in a sack with all the other lost things—
bobby pins, crayons, my mother's bracelet.

I imagined him rooting through his treasures,
grimy fingers stroking my missing Barbie's hair.
His hooked nose, pock-marks, tattered cap—
but the truth is, I'd never really seen Mr. Gull.

My sister had. He'd knocked at the door and
she watched as my father answered.
Mr. Gull spoke in low tones, she said, and when
he took off his hat, a river of sand poured onto the porch.

I've always watched for sand,
and for shadows on the wall.

And I know that when my love tugs on my arm
to draw me out of nightmares,
it is Mr. Gull, dirt under his fingernails,
who pulls on the other side.

How We Said Goodbye

for Alana

Before the operation, we laughed
because Äiti was drugged and hilarious:

declaring that your preschool teacher
had looked like Shrek, giggling as

she tried to tell us stories we'd
never heard before.

It was the last time we three
were awake together. She looked at us

clustered at her bedside
and sighed, *my girls,* as though

she knew it was the end but
wished to keep it quiet—her final

secret in a motherhood full of
truths she did not want to tell.

Then she was swollen and
strange looking. We sang to her

in case she could hear us,
a Karelian lullaby she used to murmur

in a thin voice when we couldn't sleep.
Now, she slept endlessly, her hands

taut and puffed like small balloons,
and I realized she was gone from us.

The smell of her hair and skin
was all that we could recognize.

I inhaled the scent in gulping breaths,
wanting to preserve it.

How odd we must have looked:
two tear-stained women, barely grown,

sniffing our mother as she died.
Was there a witness? I think it was only us.

In my Living Room

for Alana, again

A small wooden table, you know the one,
smudged with crayon wax and dried glue,
two tiny chairs pushed in, each top rail
painted with a faded blue horse.

Your nephews have covered its surface
with stickers and playdoh crumbs,
not knowing it was once unsullied,
not knowing it was meant for high tea.

I should tell them how Grandma Mina's
blue and gold shift was a gown on you,
how we filled Äiti's china tea-set with
chocolate milk and sugar cubes.

I never minded how the lace gloves itched or
how tightly you tied the ribbon under my chin.
It was worth it to sip sweetly,
Äiti peeking in the playroom to smile at us,

call us Lady Sarah or Allison, whoever you said
we were that day. She kept this table for years,
even when she moved out of the old house.
She saved everything but herself, threw out

only glass empties long after the doctor
told her she couldn't drink. But this table,
stored and cared for, is something I have now—
a sturdy thing. Sometimes I glance and see us

sitting there: your ankles crossed, straw hat
sliding down my small forehead. Our teacups
are empty and all around us are ghosts,
shadows of what we did not yet know.

Nephew

for Alana, a third time

Waiting for his arrival, I think:
he will be one of *us*.

Tonight—as sleet streaks
hospital windows,

our duo (you and me—
like two soft cats) will grow.

He comes from your body
that knows stories I know,
fingers that remember

the contents of old desk drawers
and how the apricot fur felt
behind our little dog's ears,

and a coffee can filled with
tiny colorful stones and feathers
that we glued to faded cardstock.

He comes from your body that is
nearly my body, that lay close to me
under blankets and sang

in a secret language
made of warm breath
and cotton

and the number two.
Or perhaps we were three,
and now we are three again.

Äiti is gone, but I'll tell you a secret
that I know, sister.
She has kissed his head,

and whispered his name and
held him, held him, held him
until he curled inside of you.

After Great Pain

A formal feeling comes, yes, like Emily said,
that wooden way you walk in the world
like your body doesn't belong to you.

When people still say *I'm sorry* all the time
and you offer mechanical nods in response.
And after that? What happens then?

The strangeness of the morning you wake up
and realize none of this has killed you.

But if someone were to open your shades,
let in sunlight, and chirp *you'll be stronger
when it's all over*, you might punch them.

Maybe you will be stronger, who knows,
but you aren't looking for
platitudes or silver linings.

You're just looking for a word, or a touch—
something to survive on,
a bridge from one moment to the next.

There's not much to do but let
the hours carry you, like they always have.
To let spring arrive, and then summer,

to watch as the yellow roses on your favorite bush
blossom, then shrink again.
Every year they come back, thorns and all.

Maybe you'll find a gold-flecked fragment
in some dark corner, and then lose it again.
Maybe you'll be okay.

Either way, the days,
inscrutable and lovely,
go on.

La Vida Futura

Where are you— that question,
months after you were gone,
still echoed in my body like a sob.

Perhaps your eternity
is a black and white photograph—
a club in Palma de Mallorca,
where a ghostly Lorenzo Santamaria
approaches the stage.

You are not a groupie, of course,
especially not in the afterlife
where for once things are all right.

He sings "Para que no me olvides,"
and its haunting notes swirl without end.
No ash falls from your cigarette,
the ice in your drink does not melt.

Specters float in and out of the room,
and you watch them, smiling.
These are the people of a future
which has already happened—

neighbors, daughters, strangers,
phantoms who lean close to you to listen,
who know you have stories to tell.

Dreaming of You

In a dream you are alive,
and since you've been gone
for a while, my brain believes
we are estranged, distant.

I never know what I've
done, what's forced this
impenetrable wedge of
years between us.

At twenty, I'd still hold your
hand at the market, still climb
into bed with you mornings
during a visit.

It's a cruel trick, really.
You stand, eating rye crackers
over the kitchen sink,
barely noticing me.

In another dream I visit
an apartment you bought
when you moved away
and didn't tell us.

Later we sit in the unfamiliar
booth of a nearby diner,
our hands on the table,
heavy with tension.

I want to reach
across laminated menus
and touch your face—
smooth and impassive.

A fluorescent bulb flickers.
There is so much
I have to tell you
before I wake up.

At the Hospital

We've been here too many times,
my father says and I agree.
But I walk quickly in hallways,
sanitize my hands, perch
on the end of his white bed
and do not consider crying.

There is another self
hiding inside of me,
who resists the elevators,
who attempts to slow my steps,
who whispers *I cannot*,
and pins my hands to my sides.

If she had her way,
I would tear out of this place,
curl up in the trunk of my car,
and pretend that the ones I love
are not capable of dying,
or imagine I don't love them at all.

Under bluish lights
in the cafeteria, I toast a bagel
and think of how calm I must look.
I am not an orphan. Not yet.

Lived Here

They told me not to move in, not directly perhaps,
but with questioning eyebrows, a touch on the arm
so many memories they sighed, *are you sure?*

I trip on things my mother loved and kept.
Once, an unexpected drawer of old radios,
a folder of envelopes stamped airmail in red.

Her shoes still occupy half of an upstairs closet:
heeled relics only, ones she wore to Halston's parties,
the rest boxed and sent away.

Years have gone, but sometimes curls of paper,
handwritten notes, surface with the clutter
a word or two in Finnish, something to remember.

In my dreams, she wants me to stay, clicks her tongue
as I stand on the basement stairs, tentative,
a crate of old linens in my arms.

Yellow Moon

The house is quiet tonight.
I step outside in search of the
honey colored moon I read about,
but there's no fat gold coin in the sky,
only clouds in thick layers, an eerie glow.

The whole world is dripping wet.
My neighbor's peonies bow their heads low,
trickling rainwater on the slick pathway.
Next door, light shines through window fog.
Someone is awake, moving in the kitchen.

Water runs in the gutters of this
house where my mother once lived.
Tonight I'm sure that if I move quickly,
at just the right moment, I might
reach out and grasp her hand.

Traveling to a New Job

I drive alongside the river for miles—
the same river where we poured your ashes

and the funereal roses and alstroemeria,
stared as their petals quivered

and were quickly carried downstream.
It was raining that afternoon,

absurdly, like some terrible movie scene
in which someone beautiful has died

and the weather turns gray and soggy
for everyone, even oblivious strangers

who are inside drinking coffee,
laughing because nothing is wrong.

Of course it's just chance. The storm that day,
this trip along the Delaware each morning.

Your love for magical thinking was lost on me.
But as I hit the road before sunrise,

dread-heavy some days, I need to imagine
you're beside me, reminding me how to breathe.

Admission

My friends are bringing
their mothers to the matinee.
Five of us, I order six tickets.
After seven years you'd think
I might remember you are gone.

I call to return the ticket and
the Telecharge operator understands,
knows that the dead are entitled
to free admission if nothing else.

I have learned to be okay without you.
Though lately, while my son
swims inside of me, opening and closing
his tiny fists, I want to ask you
what it was like to carry me.

At the show—where will I sit?
Next to a stranger, perhaps, or
flanked by someone else's mother
and an empty chair.

It doesn't matter.
When the theater is dark and quiet,
I'll press a hand to my belly—
not really afraid, not really alone at all.

Delaware

After heavy rains, she'd eye the water,
worry that somehow it would
overflow its banks and come
creeping to our house, seep
through bedroom doors.

Now my mother is part of the river.
Her ashes have scattered and sunk
to the silty bottom, where eels
hide in clusters of underwater vines.
The current, without pity, rushes over her.

I would ask her—if I could,
what place there is beyond fear,
beyond days that feel like a breath
caught endlessly in the throat.
A place with no clocks, no heartbeats.

I would ask her—but she cannot answer,
nor unwrinkle my brow with a cool hand.
It used to be that I couldn't find her,
but now she is the part of me that
swells, that spills over.

For Äiti

You are alive but only when I sleep,
and even so my dreams of you are rare.
We're marked by loss and not by what we keep.

The River Grief is wide and it runs deep.
It flows just like our blood, our breath, the air
You were alive and then I watched you sleep.

Time carried me, I felt the hours creep.
The child I was has gone—she is nowhere.
We're changed by loss and marked by what we keep

repeating, though I know that talk is cheap.
Your records played and I watched from the stairs.
You came alive, you thought I was asleep.

My headphones on instead of counting sheep,
I'm just like you—I wonder if I dare
remark that loss is always what we keep

returning to, a touchstone, a great sweep
of memories (think of you braiding my hair.)
We are alive—I sing my boys to sleep,
not marked by loss, but just by what they keep.

Alexa Gutter is a middle school teacher, poet, and mother. She was named poet laureate of Bucks County, Pennsylvania in 2013. The daughter of a Finnish mother and a father born as a Jewish refugee in China, she often explores her heritage and ties to the past in her poetry. She currently lives in West Chester, Pennsylvania with her family. Her website is *AlexaGutter.com*.

www.ingramcontent.com/pod-product-compliance
Lightning Source LLC
Chambersburg PA
CBHW022058080426
42734CB00009B/1401